Old MURRAYFIELD and COLTBRIDGE

by
Robin Sherman

HAYMARKET TERRACE, EDINBURGH.

P&W.M.Ltd

The western end of Haymarket Terrace looking towards the city centre, with the eastern gateway to Donaldson's School on the left and Magdala Crescent branching off beyond it. This point could be considered to be the 'gateway' to Roseburn and Murrayfield, as West Coates begins immediately to the west of Magdala Crescent. Haymarket Terrace ends at West Coates Church, which was built on open farmland in 1870 and demolished in 1962 (today the Apex Hotel stands at this location). Like the church, the dwellings on the right have also been removed and this site is presently occupied by the large glass-fronted Donaldson House. Judging by the number of 'To Let' notices, its tenants are frequently subject to change.

© Robin Sherman 2003
First published in the United Kingdom, 2003,
by Stenlake Publishing
Telephone / Fax 01290 551122
Printed by Cordfall Ltd, Glasgow, G21 2QA

ISBN 1 84033 283 2

The publishers regret that they cannot supply
~~copies of any~~ y pictures featured in this book.

By the same author:
ɔn, Grange, Liberton & Gilmerton

FURTHER READING

ooks listed below were used by the author during his research. None of them are
ble from Stenlake Publishing. Those interested in finding out more are advised to
:t their local bookshop or reference library.

-*Lothian Village*, G. Upton Selway
rphine: A Pictorial History of a Midlothian Village, W. G. Dey, FRIBA
ɔrstorphine Heirloom, D. M. Thomson
rphine Notes, The Corstorphine Trust
rphine Public Hall Movement 1889, Leslie Nobbs MBE
!'s Old and New Edinburgh, James Grant
ɪrgh and Glasgow Railway Guidebook, Martin & Maclean
;MT to Eastern Scottish, D. L. G. Hunter
ic Corstorphine and Roundabout (Vols. 1 to 4), A. S. Cowper
st Picture Shows, Edinburgh, Brendon Thomas
:sque Notes of an Edinburgh Suburb, Murrayfield Residents Association
ɪce Names of Edinburgh, Stuart Harris
ɔntres: Edinburgh, A. J. Mullay
Destiny – A Brief History of Donaldson's College, George Montgomery
Edinburgh in Pictures, Charles J. Smith
f the Edinburgh Zoo, T. H. Gillespie FRSE
ɪmways of Eastern Scotland, J. C. Gillham and R. J. S. Wiseman
ɪrgh Zoo 90th anniversary brochure, The Royal Zoological Society of Scotland

INTRODUCTION

This book comprises a tour commencing at the gates of Donaldson's School for the Deaf and leading from there through Roseburn and Coltbridge. It continues via Murrayfield, where the route reaches as far north as Ravelston Dykes before heading along Corstorphine Road, through Saughtonhall and Balgreen and on to the zoo. Corstorphine is the final destination, with the locations featured there centred mainly on St John's Road and to the south of it. The area covered reaches almost as far west as Drum Brae roundabout.

It was not until the 1860s that serious building development began along the old Glasgow Road beyond Haymarket; previously it had been a poorly-surfaced rural track bordered by farms and grassland. After reaching the hamlet of Coltbridge, the road threaded its way between Corstorphine Loch to the south and Corstorphine Hill to the north, until the loch was drained during the eighteenth century. Indeed, so intermittently rough and marshy was the road surface between Coltbridge and Corstorphine that until the eighteenth century the loch was often the preferred means of transporting goods from the former to the latter. On the road, even light horse-drawn vehicles could become bogged down after heavy rains, whilst many a cartwheel was broken when the going was firm. As a result, Corstorphine, the most westerly district covered in this book, was not readily accessible from the city and was somewhat isolated until the nineteenth century.

The economy of **Roseburn** was originally fuelled by farming and dairying and by several mills on the Water of Leith. The Russell family (whose name lives on in the title of a key road, Russell Road) owned at least three mills as far back as the sixteenth century. Known as Dalry Mills, these were purchased from George Kincaid by Mungo Russell in 1576. As Edinburgh City Treasurer, Russell then built Roseburn House in 1582 (the house's door lintel bears this date) on the Dalry Mills property. The name Roseburn originated in the early eighteenth century and probably derives from the mill lade, which was perhaps rose-bordered. It was the building boom of the latter half of the nineteenth and the early twentieth century, coupled with the construction of the huge Heriot brewing complex by John Jeffrey in 1862, which created modern Roseburn (although the entire brewery site is now occupied by Roseburn Maltings, a private residential development).

Coltbridge owes its name to a medieval crossing on the Water of Leith. 'Colt' may originally derive from the old Scots word *cote*, meaning a cottage or shelter. Some have reasoned that it might also relate to the land of Coates, just up the hill to the east, although there is no concrete evidence to support this.

Murrayfield, on the other hand, quite clearly obtained its name as a result of the arrival of Archibald Murray of Cringletie (near Peebles) in 1733. He purchased much of the land in the area, then known as Nisbet Park, from the Nisbets of Dean for £40,000 Scots, and built his fine house at the top of the hill: it still stands at the upper end of Murrayfield Avenue and is now Murrayfield House Nursing Home. Archibald's son, Alexander, succeeded him in 1773, by which time the area was commonly referred to as Murrayfield.

Conversely, the precise origin of the name **Corstorphine** is lost in the mists of time, although there are four main theories as to why it is so-called. Early records quote the name as Crostorphin, and three of the contenders for the derivation accept that the first syllable refers to a cross. There the harmony ends, however, for one theory considers that the cross relates to a river crossing, another to a stone cross and the third to a small gold example.

Corstorphine's early settlers probably chose this strategic site because it was close to an ancient road crossing on a strip of land between two lochs (later to become known as Corstorphine Loch and Gogar Loch). This land was divided by a shallow burn, which flowed between the two lochs, over which there was definitely a crossing. It has been suggested that the latter half of the name derives from an association with Thorfinn, Earl of Orkney and grandson of King Malcolm II (954–1034), who perhaps crossed the river here, giving 'Cross Thorfinn'. Another theory suggests that there was an early Christian stone cross in the area, and that this had been erected by an Archdeacon of Lothian called Torphin. The name Torphin certainly has Lothian associations, for it has been given to one of the Pentland hills. The third derivation is a little more fanciful (perhaps even far-fetched!), and suggests that a gold cross was gifted to the old parish church by a Norman nobleman. This relic would have been a *croix d'or fin*, or 'cross of fine gold'.

The fourth conjecture does not concern a cross at all but is, instead, inspired by the Gaelic language. *Coire* means a hollow, *stoir* is a flight of steps and *fionn* or *phin* is Gaelic for white, giving 'The hollow with the white steps'. It has been suggested that these steps could have led down into a depression and been made from white stone or, alternatively, being situated in a marshy area between the two lochs, low-lying mists and dampness could have helped create the whiteness. It is impossible to say which, if any, definition may be correct, and doubtless assertions could be made to justify the merits of one theory over another. Readers will have to make their own choices!

With the passing of time, Corstorphine has not only lost the derivation of its name but also its loch and castle, and is now a densely populated residential suburb. I hope that the following pages will bring back some forgotten but pleasant memories for those who browse through this small book.

Born at 7 West Bow on 10 December 1751, James Donaldson made his fortune in his family's bookselling and publishing businesses in Edinburgh's High Street. The shop was situated in Salamander Land, on the site where the former police station was later built between Old Fishmarket Close and Parliament Square. When James died on 19 October 1830, he left just over £124,000 from his fortune (equivalent to almost £20 million in today's terms) to finance the building of a school. Designed by Edinburgh's foremost architect, William H. Playfair (1790–1857), the building was erected on land purchased from George Heriot's trust in 1833. On 30 August 1850, just prior to opening in October that year, Queen Victoria visited the school. She expressed her admiration for the building and was said to have remarked that 'It is finer than some of my Scottish Palaces', perhaps hinting that she would have liked it for her own use. According to local folklore, she was greatly put out because it was not offered to her. By 1880, deaf children outnumbered those with hearing at this co-educational institution, and in 1938 it became Donaldson's School for the Deaf when it amalgamated with the Edinburgh Institution for the Deaf and Dumb in Henderson Row. Time marches on, however, and as this book goes to print the building has just been sold to a property developer for conversion into luxury flats. The price paid equates, in real terms, with the original cost of the building, so it seems the developer has obtained a bargain.

Murrayfield station at Roseburn, with the rooftops of the houses in Wester Coates Terrace just visible in the background. Opened in 1879 by the Caledonian Railway Company, this line, running from Leith North to Dalry Middle junction was closed by the authorities on 30 April 1962, though plans are now being considered for its partial reinstatement as a tramway. Hauled by locomotive 0-4-4T No. 55124, the train depicted here (the Pentland-Tinto Express) was a rail enthusiasts' special and one of the very last passenger trains to use the route. This class of locomotive saw duty over many years on the rail-tracks of Scotland, having been introduced prior to the First World War.

In the early years of the twentieth century, a craze for roller skating arrived on Britain's shores from the USA. Rinks were built in cities all over the United Kingdom and this postcard, sent by a rink manager on 11 August 1909, bears the sender's address: The Edinburgh Skating Rink Co., Ltd., Russell Road. Uniformed staff were employed to assist beginners in this bruise-fraught pastime, although female skaters were probably quite well-protected by their long skirts, cushioned with numerous petticoats. A little over a decade after despatch of the postcard, roller skating had lost its appeal. The premises were then taken over by the Scottish Motor Traction Co., and became a part of their commercial vehicle depot at a time when public transport was experiencing significant growth. The notice in the background of this picture reads: 'This skating rink is not yet completed and never will be, as we will be continually adding new improvements'!

The land now occupied by Roseburn Park used to be a rather insalubrious, swampy area on the edge of the Water of Leith. This was filled in and levelled by the city council in 1891, but unfortunately still has a propensity for serious flooding when the river is in spate. After reclamation, the ground was leased for recreational purposes and the Edinburgh Polo Club (founded in 1880) moved there, stabling its ponies at Russell Road. In 1898 the city purchased about ten acres of land adjoining the polo ground from the Balfour family of Balburnie and turned this into Roseburn Park. Sporting facilities were developed including golf with the founding of Roseburn Golf Club in 1901. Later, the game of rugby asserted its authority with the erection of Murrayfield Stadium in the 1920s on the old polo ground and part of the golf course. The stadium opened in a blaze of glory on 21 March 1925 with Scotland playing England. The home team won 14–11 before 70,000 spectators and in doing so clinched the Grand Slam, Triple Crown and Calcutta Cup in one fell swoop. It was to be almost 60 years before that feat was repeated (in the 1983–4 season).

The junction of Roseburn Terrace (foreground), Corstorphine Road (left), Murrayfield Avenue (background) and Murrayfield Place (right) photographed from an elevated vantage point. In the 1920s the shops in Murrayfield Place included A. Smith, ladies and gents hairdressers (there is still a hairdressing business in this location in 2003 with the ultra-modern name of www.idhair.com) and James Waldie & Sons, coal merchant. The latter was one of many such businesses dotted around Edinburgh at a time when coal was an essential commodity. In those days deliveries from local shops were mainly made by horse or hand-drawn carts or bicycles.

This view looks towards Roseburn Terrace (right) and Murrayfield Place (left). The terrace of houses which lies to the left, seemingly halfway along Murrayfield Place, is actually in Coltbridge Avenue. This was built in 1869 and the local Murrayfield post office was housed at No. 6 until it later moved next door to No. 8, where it remains to this day. The white cottage with the pitched roof close to the tram is one of three which was built on the instructions of George Pape (d. 1854). He married Jessie Paterson, whose family owned Coltbridge House at the bottom of Murrayfield Avenue, immediately below the Church of the Good Shepherd, designed by Sir Robert Lorimer. As well as the house, she also brought twelve acres of land in the vicinity to the marriage, including the riparian Green Grass Brae on which the trio of cottages was subsequently erected. A plaque on the wall states that 'These cottages were built for the use of three poor widows in all time coming'. Known not surprisingly as Pape's Cottages, they are now privately-owned dwellings, despite the declaration on the plaque.

Coltbridge Terrace appears much the same today as it did a century ago when this postcard was produced, although the trees are now bigger and the traffic heavier. Until the street was built up and given its present name *c*.1875, the road from Coltbridge to Ravelston Dykes was known as Skinner's Loan, after the skinners who worked at Coltbridge in the local leather industry. Several centuries ago, as a consequence of its proximity to the eastern end of the old Corstorphine Loch, Coltbridge had a well-used water-borne transport system connecting it with Corstorphine and its castle. Indeed, funds to maintain the lamp on the eastern wall of Corstorphine Kirk (by which travellers were guided on dank and misty nights) were raised in Coltbridge until the early eighteenth century through rental of 'ane aiker of land lying bewest the Cowes Brigge upon ye south side of ye little house that stands by ye wayside'. (Cowes Brigge seems to have been an even earlier name for Coltbridge, and perhaps related to the animals used in the production of leather.) This rented area became known as Lampacre, and also helped subsidise the salary of the Corstorphine schoolmaster. The plot concerned was a triangular-shaped strip of land on the northern bank of the Water of Leith, between what is today 37 Corstorphine Road and Riverside Crescent, further to the west. There were other such 'lampacres' in Edinburgh and its environs; for example in Corstorphine and Gogar Burn.

At the top end of Coltbridge Terrace lies Garscube Terrace, which begins close to the point where this picture was taken and was built over the upper section of Skinner's Loan. Horse-drawn delivery carts are seen on their afternoon rounds here, with the one closest to the camera belonging to Robert Duff, fruit & potato merchants, Corstorphine. The entry immediately beyond the gates in the right foreground now provides the main access to St George's School for Girls. On the left a group of men are digging up the road. Some things never change!

Coltbridge Hall was built in 1875 as a large private residence, and in 1900 was taken over by a private ladies' school (Lansdowne School) which was looking to expand. This was run by the Misses Fenton and Emerson and was formerly housed in a more modest building in Lansdowne Crescent, nearer the West End. Coltbridge Hall was thus renamed Lansdowne. In 1976 Lansdowne School amalgamated with the nearby St George's School for Girls.

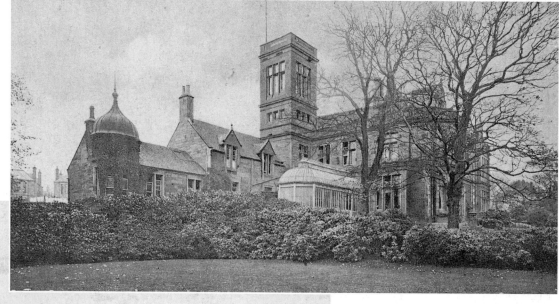

St George's School for Girls moved in 1914 from smaller premises in Melville Street to this building, designed by the architect Balfour Paul, in Garscube Terrace. I have an affinity with the school because my daughter is a former pupil and has recently been appointed as a teacher there. Presently the school provides education for just over 950 pupils, 52 of whom are boarders. This postcard dates from shortly after its opening.

Murrayfield Avenue led up to the family home of Archibald Murray, who purchased much of the land in this area in 1733 from wealthy local landowners, the Nisbets of Dean. At that time the Nisbets lived in a grand house whose gardens now form Dean Cemetery, where the remains of many famous Edinburgh personages lie along with parts of the old house itself. Archibald Murray's son, Alexander, succeeded him in 1773, by which time the lands were commonly known as Murrayfield. He acquired the Henderland Estate from Lord Queensberry and when he became Lord of Session, took the title Lord Henderland.

Murrayfield House, Edinburgh.

It was soon after completing his purchase of land in the area that Archibald built Murrayfield House, which at that time must have had fine unobstructed views in all directions. This house nearly met its end in 1915 when it was proposed that Murrayfield Avenue be extended through to Ravelston Dykes. Fortunately it was then occupied by two maiden ladies of importance and influence: Miss Isabella Grace Pratt Chalmers (daughter of the founder of Merchiston Castle School, and niece of Dr Thomas Chalmers, who led the Disruption in 1843) and the Hon. Constance Shore, daughter of Lord Teignmouth. They organised a petition which was so successful that the new road was forced to take a dog-leg to the right and reach the Dykes by the creation of Succoth Avenue. Today the building is Murrayfield House Nursing Home.

MURRAYFIELD AVENUE, EDINBURGH.

A century-old view from close to the gates of Murrayfield House, looking back down Murrayfield Avenue. There used to be a small loch adjacent to the grounds of the house, sited within the triangular area framed today by Succoth Avenue and Gardens and Ravelston Dykes.

Murrayfield Gardens, seen from the bottom of the hill close to Corstorphine Road. During the Second World War Donaldson's School was surrounded by barbed wire and used as a prisoner of war camp for captured Germans and Italians. Parties of these prisoners were organised to carry out labouring duties, such as road digging and cable laying, and were sometimes seen marching along the main road on their way to work in Corstorphine or its environs. Given that the main aim of many British POWs was to escape from German custody, I often wonder why their counterparts, held in less secure circumstances, did not show the same zeal for freedom.

MURRAYFIELD GARDENS

Kingsburgh Road, Murrayfield

Both of the streets seen here – Abinger Gardens and Kingsburgh Road – were built at the beginning of the last century on the estate belonging to the Campbells of Succoth, as was Ormidale Terrace, illustrated on the following page. The street names chosen derive from luminaries in the legal profession. James Scarlett was Attorney General before becoming Lord Abinger in 1835. He was also the son-in-law of Sir Ilay Campbell, owner of the land on which the street was laid out. Kingsburgh Road was named for the Lord Chief Justice, Lord Kingsburgh, whilst Ormidale Terrace was named after Robert Macfarlane, a well-known Scottish judge who became Lord Ormidale in 1862.

Abinger Gardens, Murrayfield

ORMIDALE TERRACE, MURRAYFIELD, EDINBURGH

Ormidale Terrace viewed from its junction with Kingsburgh Road. At its foot, on the corner with Abinger Gardens, is Murrayfield Church of Scotland where my mother worshipped during the final twenty years of her life. She was also a member of the church's social group, The Lighthearts. In the more distant past, the first occupants to move into the second house on the right in this view were the Fairbairn family, about whom more details are provided on page 27.

"AULD REEKIE" FROM CORSTORPHINE HILL TOWER, EDINBURGH

One of the very best views of the city is obtained from atop Corstorphine Hill, and in recent years at Hogmanay it has become a popular vantage point from which to view the synchronised city-wide firework displays. Corstorphine Hill Tower, from where this picture was taken, was erected in 1871 by William McFie of Clermiston House to commemorate the centenary of the birth of Sir Walter Scott. Murrayfield Golf Club, whose new clubhouse opened in July 1912, can be seen in the foreground of this 1950s view. The Campbells of Succoth purchased the estate south of Ravelston Dykes in 1816 and many of the streets shown in this picture were named after properties owned by the family; these include Crarae, Cumlodden, Lennel, Garscube and Succoth. Craigleith Crescent and Blinkbonny Road can also be spotted. Much of Craigleith View has yet to be built within the green area beyond the Ravelston Garden flats to the extreme left of the picture.

Saughtonhall Drive at its junction with Saughtonhall Avenue, with Jenner's Depository in the distance on the right. The four shops on the corner are still recognisable today; all the businesses have changed, of course, but the one on the extreme left continues to function as a newsagent/confectioner, having, in the meantime, extended into the premises of Chalmers the chemist. Gilchrist the grocer has now become Mitchell's fruit and veg, whilst the former butcher's shop is now home to an IT consultancy firm.

The view from the foot of Saughtonhall Drive looking back towards the junction from which the previous picture was taken. Behind the photographer – and out of view – is Jenner's Depository, a well-known landmark since it was erected as a storage warehouse for the famous Princes Street store. Another business which has continued to operate from the same premises for the best part of a century can be seen on the left – St Cuthbert's Co-operative Association, now Scotmid. Many branches have since been closed but this one still provides a welcome service for the neighbourhood, despite the fact that the 'divi' is no longer paid, although there is a move to try and have it reinstated. Note the horse trough at the roadside and the delivery carts near the stationary bus.

Saughtonhall Drive, Edinburgh.

A very empty-looking Balgreen Avenue seen before the left (south) side had been built up with houses. This postcard was sent on 17 February 1911 and the small shop on the right continues to do business today. The name Balgreen may derive from the glacial gravel which previously formed the shoreline of the old Corstorphine Loch and was to be found on farmland here; *baile griain* is Gaelic for 'gravelly farm'.

The 'Saughtons' (derived from *sauch*, an old word for the willow tree) are all on the other side of Balgreen Road. This postcard of Saughton Grove, sent in 1935, was purchased at the shop illustrated above, run at the time by M. & E. Lawrie.

Balgreen Halt was where the Corstorphine spur line, built in 1902 by the North British Railway, left the Edinburgh/Glasgow main line. In this 1967 photograph, a Cravens DMU (Diesel Multiple Unit) has stopped on its way to Waverley while on the distant horizon Murrayfield Stadium and the spires of St Mary's Cathedral can be seen. This halt was originally created to facilitate the movement of passenger traffic to and from the hugely-successful Scottish National Exhibition, which took place at the nearby house and grounds of Saughton Hall in 1908.

The decades on either side of 1900 were when the greatest of the international trade exhibitions were held, and from May to October 1908 Edinburgh staged what was one of the most memorable in the UK. During its six-month duration 3,351,331 people attended, and on the final day 53,563 passed through the gates (the highest single-day attendance was 65,140). When the bars closed early on that last evening, riots ensued and police reinforcements had to be quickly summoned. A selection of large purpose-built halls was erected, amongst which were a Music and Conference Hall, Machinery Hall, Art Galleries and a Palace of Industries; there was even a Baby Incubator Hall. Many countries occupied their own pavilions promoting their folklore, trade goods and artisan work. The fairground was the most popular venue and some of the rides can be seen in this view, including, in the background, the Water Chute. Other favourites were the Figure of Eight Railway and the Hall of Laughter. The popularity of this exhibition, with its huge attendances, was said to have provided the motivation for the subsequent development of the zoo.

The first 'zoological gardens' in Edinburgh were opened to the public in 1839 on a site adjoining the villa of Broughton Park, towards the eastern end of Claremont Street. This house was the former country home built by James Donaldson, the benefactor of Donaldson's School. In 1850 the zoo was authorised to add the prefix 'royal' by Queen Victoria, but did not survive for much longer and closed around 1858. The present zoo was the brainchild of an Edinburgh lawyer, T. H. Gillespie, and opened on 22 July 1913, a small portion of the funding having been derived from an interest-enhanced deposit, initially created after the winding-up of the previous zoo. The large gateway and pair of stone falcons on either side of the clock originally formed the entrance to Falcon Hall in Morningside. This fine home was built c.1815 by Alexander Falconar and taken down in 1901. John Bartholemew, the famous cartographer, was its final owner.

With its steeply-sloping and sunny south-facing 82 acre estate, Corstorphine Hill House was deemed the most suitable and reasonably-priced location for the new zoo. Purchased in 1911 for £17,000, it was chosen over several other possible sites in Murrayfield and Corstorphine, including the most favoured, Belmont, which was rendered unviable because the Hope family, who owned it, wanted £40,000 for it (close to £4 million in today's terms). The original Corstorphine Hill House was built by the Keith family and dates from 1793. It was considerably extended in the 1890s by the then owners, the Macmillan family, whose company, Melrose Tea, helped generate the family fortune. Now it provides facilities for zoo members and incorporates restaurants, a bar and rooms for use on social occasions such as the annual Christmas Carol service. Pressure on the fine old house was relieved in 1976 with the opening of the purpose-built education centre, which hosts classes for about 50,000 children and quite a few adults annually, a tremendous educational achievement.

Opened in 1867 on five acres of ground purchased from the 102 acre Meadowhouse Farm, the Convalescent Hospital (background) was financed by William Seton Brown, who considered it important for hospital patients' recovery to be enhanced by sun, rest and recuperation. He declared that he wished to provide for those patients who needed 'more complete restoration to health but who cannot be allowed longer to remain [at the Royal Infirmary]'. Statistics for the year to 1 October 1912 revealed that '1,323 patients had the benefit of a stay here before returning home. Of these, 925 remained for three weeks, or longer.' Such treatment contrasts markedly with today's short stays in hospital! Across the road, the Children's Home designed in the Elizabethan style by James Jerdan still exists as the Scottish headquarters for Barnardo's. In 1911 this became the Widowers' Children's Home, specifically for children who had lost their mothers (their fathers had to contribute to the cost of their upkeep). Corstorphine Hill House (now the members' house at the zoo) can just be seen among the trees to the extreme right. The large Forestry Commission offices were constructed on the site of the old Meadowhouse farmhouse, which was derelict by 1974.

The new zoo provided the impetus for an extension of the corporation bus and tram routes beyond Saughtonhall. This 1920s photograph shows, on the left, tram No. 213, an open-topped cable car that was converted to electric traction at the beginning of the 1920s and provided with a roof at the same time. The tram is standing at the Murrayfield terminus (the most westerly point on Edinburgh's tramway system at this time) and a group of people are in the process of transferring to the two Leyland buses on the left (the one in the foreground is S 9310) which will take them on to the zoo.

This 32-seat Thornycroft bus (SG 8033), destined for Bathgate, provided a service to and from the zoo, as did the Corstorphine-bound tram immediately behind it. The latter was another car which had been converted from cable traction when the route was electrified in 1923. The bus was operated by SMT (Scottish Motor Traction Co. Ltd.) of Edinburgh, which at that time was extending its services from the capital to various outlying towns and villages.

Sent in June 1906, this postcard shows Kaimes Road at an early stage of its development, long before it was extended up to Cairnmuir in the 1930s. Edinburgh School of Gardening for Women can be seen at the top of the road, close to its junction with Old Kirk Road. This was founded by Misses Barker and Morrison, who were keen suffragettes. At the outbreak of the First World War, the lady gardeners became land workers, taking over the roles of men who had gone off to fight. The road is well-named, for the old Scots word *kame* means a ridge or the crest of a hill. The same group of houses can be seen in the background of the next picture.

This personal photograph has been printed as a postcard for the Cairns family, two of whom are proudly depicted sitting in their Argyll car at the foot of a verdant Belgrave Road, looking across to Kaimes Road. Although postmarked 1905, the photograph was taken at least two years earlier, as St Anne's Parish Church, which celebrated its centenary in April 2003, is not present in the picture. In its early days, services were held in a prefabricated 398 seat 'tin kirk', and at that time much of Corstorphine Hill was cloaked in field and forest. David Cairns was a wealthy shipowner at the start of the twentieth century, whose company had its offices in Constitution Street, Leith. His daughter, Lily, married Jamie Fairbairn, a printer, in 1904 and they moved to Ormidale Terrace just after the houses were built.

A Gloucester DMU calls at Pinkhill station, the stopping point for those who wished to visit the zoo. When it opened in 1913, the tramway did not extend as far as Pinkhill and the rail-link formed by the spur line between Corstorphine and Haymarket West junction was crucial in bringing people to meet the animals.

A Gresley Class V3 2-6-2T locomotive, No. 67615, steams out of Pinkhill station with a passenger service on the final stage of its journey to Corstorphine, while some disgorged passengers wend their way homewards along Traquair Park East, running parallel to the railway line. The view is still easily recognisable, despite the fact that the railway line closed long ago and the trackbed is now overgrown with greenery.

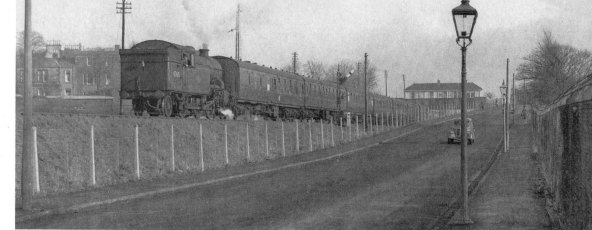

558

17 SOUTH FREDERICK STREET,
EDINBURGH.

William Forbes Esq
Lochcote Bathgate

R. B. LAIRD & SONS

Bought of ~~Downie & Laird,~~

Nurserymen, Seedsmen & Florists.

NURSERIES;

FLORISTS TO THE QUEEN.

ROYAL WINTER GARDENS, WEST COATES, ADJOINING DONALDSON'S HOSPITAL,
AND
PINKHILL, NEAR CORSTORPHINE.

A. RITCHIE & SON, EDIN.

A look at maps of Corstorphine and Murrayfield in the early years of the twentieth century reveals a number of plant nurseries dotted at various sites between the eastern and western extremities of the area covered in this book. To the west of Corstorphine, adjacent to Meadow Place Road, was Vine Cottage Nursery; in the village, near the dovecot was another smaller nursery. East along the main road past Kaimes Road and the Convalescent Hospital were two pairs of large nurseries facing each other across the road: Pinkhill and Meadow Park; and Beechhill and Beechwood Mains. Other smaller enterprises included Osbourne, Murrayfield, Ladywell and Meadowbank Nurseries, and the Edinburgh School of Gardening for Women. At the easternmost point of the area was West Coates, a large nursery with extensive glasshouses, situated adjacent to Donaldson's School. Today no nurseries remain in the area, their sites having been developed for housing. Founded in 1848 by John Downie and R. B. Laird, the firm of Downie & Laird, Nurserymen, Seedsmen and Florists had premises in South Frederick Street as well as nurseries at West Coates and Pinkhill. The West Coates site lay in an area roughly bounded by Magdala Crescent and Place, Coates Garden and Haymarket Terrace. A large expanse of glasshouses stood there and became known as the Royal Winter Gardens; they occupied the site for 45 years before it was developed for housing. In 1882 Messrs Downie and Laird parted company, with R. B. Laird taking over the entire existing business and J. Downie setting up on his own account. The Pinkhill site was acquired from the Mackie family who had established a nursery on the land in the early nineteenth century (the name Pinkhill is thought to have come from the pink of the rhododendrons growing on the hillside). The nurseries extended to 50 acres and remained in the Laird family's ownership until the site was bought by the Royal Zoological Society, which in 1972 sold it to the Post House Hotel. At Meadow Park on the opposite side of the road from Pinkhill, and at Beechwood Mains about a quarter of a mile nearer Edinburgh, the Lairds owned tree nurseries. John Downie remained a nurseryman and seedsman after the split with his partner, with a shop in Princes Street and nurseries at Rosemount and Beechhill. The latter occupied this site for the first part of the twentieth century.

The main building at this, the second Corstorphine station (opened on 1 February 1902), lay at right-angles to the tracks behind the buffer stops. (The first station was built in 1842 on the main line to Glasgow, and was situated just under a mile south of Corstorphine at Saughton Mains Street.) Many will recall the topiary at the side entrance to the platform, just out of the picture to the left, which at one time was shaped to represent a dog. The city council's lack of foresight in sanctioning the closure of this route to Waverley station in 1967 is surpassed only by its decision to permit beautiful old buildings to be torn down in Princes Street around the same period; these were replaced with concrete and glass monstrosities. Travellers could reach Waverley from Corstorphine in eleven minutes, irrespective of the time of day, and it was a well-used route which – had it been preserved – would have substantially relieved the passenger transport problems along at least one of Edinburgh's congested traffic arteries. Latterly mothers with prams could wheel their offspring directly from platform onto train, a much-welcomed facility. In 1958 a daily through train to North Berwick was introduced, and this picture shows a Metro–Cammell DMU ready for departure on this service.

The land on which Traquair Park was built in 1903 was owned by the Traquair Dickson family, hence the street's name. This family name came about with the marriage in the 1840s between Elizabeth Traquair, the daughter of an Edinburgh builder, and a Saughton farmer named John Dickson. The cars in the picture would have been shaken to pieces had they had to withstand the many steep speed bumps now ornamenting the road.

TRAQUAIR PARK, CORSTORPHINE.

This rural view shows Glebe Road (to the left) leading down to Corstorphine Parish Church, surrounded by its headstone-filled graveyard. What was at the time the 'new' library building can also be seen. This was opened in 1904 with financial assistance from Andrew Carnegie, who donated £1,000, and was built hard against the public hall (constructed in 1892 at a cost £1,453, 4s). The new library replaced an earlier and more primitive facility which had been in existence since at least 1838. Today Corstorphine Library has moved to adjacent premises and the 1904 building is currently occupied by a firm of accountants and another of surveyors. In the meantime the hall has become the Corstorphine Youth and Community Centre.

At the beginning of the eleventh century it was recorded that a chapel belonging to Norman, Sheriff of Berwick, stood on or near the site of the present Corstorphine Parish Church. A little later King David I (1084–1153) bestowed the chapel, as part of the adjoining Church of St Cuthbert, on the Abbey of Holyrood. Later still the parish church was dedicated to St Mary, and in 1429 Adam, first Lord Forrester, founded the present church, then dedicated to St John the Baptist. The precise position of these former churches has not been established, but in common with other ancient religious sites the present church building (which over the years has seen many expansions, alterations and renovations) was probably built on top of, or very close to, the earlier places of worship. An interesting feature is the flight of two steps leading down into the church nave, representing the descent into the Jordan where Jesus and his believers were baptised by St John. A niche on the eastern gable, which can still be seen to this day, held the lamp which provided a guide to night-time travellers crossing the marshy land east of the church or the more distant Corstorphine Loch.

Saughton Road North leads into the distance along what was once the bed of Corstorphine Loch. The row of houses in the left foreground forms Sycamore Terrace, while just beyond it, also on the left, is the entrance to Meadowhouse Road, on the corner of which a modern block of flats now stands. Dovecot Road can be seen leading off to the right across the main road. Dating from the sixteenth century, the circular Corstorphine Castle dovecot provided fresh pigeon meat in winter with its 1,060 nests ranged from floor to ceiling behind a wall which was almost four feet thick. Just to the east of this dovecot grew a famous old sycamore. Originally one of a number of trees lining the main entranceway to the long-vanished castle, it lived to be at least four centuries old. Indeed, tradition had it that a monk returning from the east in the fifteenth century brought the sycamore saplings with him.

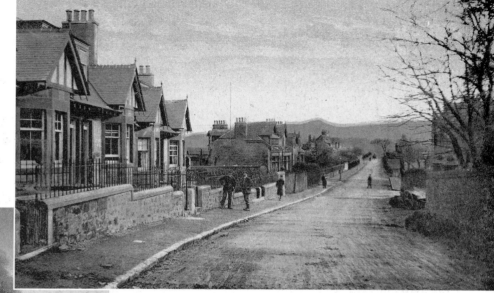

Under the considerable branch network of this sycamore tree, the hard-drinking and smooth-womanising 2nd Lord Forrester (eleventh master of Corstorphine Castle) met his end on the night of 26 August 1679. (In fact he was not a Forrester at all, but James Baillie, husband of the fourth daughter of George, the heirless 1st Lord.) Returning with a stagger to his step from the Black Bull Inn, he was met by a wronged female relative, Christian Nimmo, who after a heated altercation failed to live up to her first name and ran him through with his own sword. More than three centuries afterwards, about 8 p.m. on a stormy Boxing Day night in 1998, Derick Fisher, who lived in the modern block of flats across the road from the tree, was well settled down for the night and watching *Gunfight at the OK Corral* on TV when an almighty crack rent the air. Realising that this had nothing to do with the on-screen gunslingers, he reached his window just as the huge sycamore came crashing to the ground, blocking the main road and almost reaching his flat. A very long life had just come to an end, but fortunately Derick's was spared!

This scenic view shows the western end of Dovecot Road at its junction with Ladywell Avenue (named after a nearby water source, Our Lady's Well) in the early years of the twentieth century. 100 years earlier this area would have formed part of the fields of Clay Cott Farm. Corstorphine Castle, built by the Forrester family on the ancient lochside, was sited 150 yards south-west of the dovecot on a plot which would have lain between 21–23 Dovecot Road and 18–20 Castle Avenue. The ancient Stank Burn, which had facilitated the draining of Corstorphine Loch, flows in the area close to the foreground, just out of the picture. Rather surprisingly, this name has nothing to do with the smell created by the effluent which used to flow into the burn; instead it comes from the French *étang*, meaning pond or pool. At the other end of Dovecot Road stood the old sycamore tree, the still-sprouting stump of which can be seen to this day in the last garden on the northern side. Christian Nimmo was beheaded in Edinburgh on 12 November 1679 after a fleeting escape from the Tolbooth dressed as a man. Following her execution, her ghost was said to haunt the area under the sycamore tree.

This was the old Clay Cott farmhouse, various tenants of which farmed the land around present-day Ladywell Avenue between St Margaret's Park and Dunsmuir Court. The name Clay Cott derives from the nature of the soil, which was mainly clay-based. Tradition has it that some of Bonnie Prince Charlie's Highland Army rested at this farmhouse on 14 September 1745 whilst their leader took respite at the nearby Dower House. Today the house can be seen on the south side of the High Street, incorporated within the much newer Claycot Park retirement complex.

LADSTONE PLACE, CORSTORPHINE.   239/31.

There is no longer a Gladstone Place at this location, and the row of houses now occupies a central section of Corstorphine High Street. (Confusion might otherwise have resulted, for Leith also has a Gladstone Place and Marchmont a Gladstone Terrace.) Despite the loss of the name, the buildings on the left remain clearly recognisable a century later, though a large tree has since grown at the entrance to Manse Road. The gateposts of the Dower House can be seen beyond Cross Cottages on the extreme right of this familiar scene, looking along the High Street to 'Irish Corner' in the distance. This area's name derives from the fact that Irish labourers lived there after they came to Edinburgh to work on the construction of the Union Canal and the railways in the first half of the nineteenth century. Its cottages stood next to the church but were taken down in 1928. By 1891 there were just 57 Irish living in Corstorphine and its environs out of a total population of 2,332. After the cottages were removed, the war memorial was transferred to the newly grassed Irish Corner site from outside the railway station, where it had stood since 1919.

Once known as Gibson Lodge after an eighteenth century owner, Dame Henrietta Watson (Lady Gibsone), this house was bought by the city council in 1923, after which it reverted to the name of the Dower House. Its gateposts were very similar to those of St Margaret's Park, further along the High Street, and it is believed that the latter formerly framed a side entrance to Corstorphine Castle known as Cross Avenue. In actual fact it is doubtful whether Gibson Lodge was ever a dower house and it may have begun life as a manse, one of three for which Sir John Forrester donated land locally. It is recorded that, as early as 1587, James Inglis lived there when it functioned as the prebendal manse. In 1765 the dwelling was greatly extended (possibly using some of the stone from the castle ruins) by its then owner, Samuel Mitchelson (an Edinburgh lawyer), who constructed a third storey. In 1792 he decided that he needed a larger home and erected Clermiston House. From the mid-nineteenth century until 1923 the Dower House was occupied by several generations of the Thomson family. Presently it accommodates the headquarters of the Corstorphine Trust and is home to its Heritage Centre. The Trust is an admirable organisation which was formed after the Second World War to preserve the best elements of Corstorphine and serve its residents. The house also plays host to the meetings of the Lothian Postcard Club on the second Friday of each month from March to December, and new members are always welcome.

ST. MARGARET'S PARK, CORSTORPHINE   D 905

The view from an upper window of the Dower House, looking across St Margaret's Park to the back gardens of the houses in Dovecot Road. Some of the homes in Orchardfield Avenue can be seen to the left. This parkland was gifted in 1915 to the parish council by the Hon. Christopher D. Brown, a wealthy American benefactor with Corstorphine connections. Bowling and tennis remain the most important recreational activities in the park, perhaps unsurprisingly when one considers the prohibitive bye-laws which were drawn up when the park was formed. These stated that no noisy pursuits were to be conducted, such as 'football or carpet beating' or meetings 'to promote political, socialist or religious causes'.

High Street, Corstorphine

This picture was taken a little further along the High Street with the Dower House gateway to the extreme right. George Smaillie, fruiterer and greengrocer, is doing his afternoon rounds whilst a passing pony and trap is in danger of disturbing the children who have lined up for the photograph. Typically, the boys have strung themselves across the road whilst the more sensible girls have stuck to the pavement. The Corstorphine Inn, established in 1886, still operates from the low building on the right behind Smaillie's cart. Further along, at the corner with Saughton Road North, lay the erstwhile Black Bull Inn.

CROSS COTTAGES. CORSTORPHINE. 239/36.

The St Margaret Park gateposts, just beyond the cottages, locate this photograph. These old houses were sited immediately across the High Street from the village school and were demolished in 1929. Called the Cross Cottages, they were named after the nearby livestock market, 'the Cross of Corstorphine', which was demarcated by five elm trees: one on each corner of a square and a fifth in the middle. The trees grew where the present school was erected and dated back to at least the seventeenth century. They were supposed to have been replaced nearby when the school originally took over the market site in 1819, but this does not appear to have happened. In 1987 the council planted some rowan trees in St Margaret's Park in recognition of the long-lost Cross. In the distance the white house which was the original Clay Cott farmhouse (reputed to have been the oldest house in Corstorphine) can just be made out. It has now been incorporated into Claycot Park, a retirement complex built in 1985.

The 'new' manse, which gave its name to Manse Road (seen here and previously known as The Slap) was completed in 1770 at a cost of £281. This included a stable for two horses as well as a byre for the same number of cows. The minister's dwelling stood on the north-eastern corner of Manse Road, at its junction with St John's Road, until it was demolished in 1959. Part of the grounds provided the site for the newer row of shops to be seen today. The trees in the middle distance on the right in this view marked the southern boundary of the manse garden, whilst those on the left were later taken down to make way for the Astoria Cinema. St Ninian's Church can just be seen in the distance. The row of houses on the right was constructed in 1884.

Astoria,
Corstorphine.

The Astoria opened for business on 1 January 1930, with its 1,228 seat interior decorated in restful autumnal colours and its screen curtains made from rose-coloured velvet decorated with gold braid. Like most of Edinburgh's 30-odd other cinemas, performances at the Astoria during the 1960s included two full-length films, Movietone News, adverts and sometimes a cartoon or short film – you got good value for money in those days. Every Saturday morning there was a children's matinee, the last one before closure (a double bill) showing *Anything for Laughs* and *Zeppelin*. The doors finally closed on 29 June 1974 with Clint Eastwood starring in *Magnum Force*. Rather appropriately, the B film was called *You Don't Know Why You Came Here*, to which could have been added, 'but you'll certainly never come again'. Derick Fisher fondly remembers his visits to this cinema in the 1950s, when he and his friends in the Scouts – and indeed in the Guides – would go as a group and afterwards head for the Valente family's Three Ks Cafe, before the boys walked the girls home. Today the cinema, with its 'chummy seats' – the stimuli to many a steamy embrace – has been replaced by the distinctly less entertaining Iceland supermarket.

Situated in St John's Road facing its junction with Manse Road, St Ninian's Church was originally built as Corstorphine Free Church, opening on Sunday 19 May 1844. Previously its growing congregation had met in temporary accommodation including a tent and a schoolroom. The original stone building was substantially renovated and expanded between 1867 and 1870, when a flat roof was converted to a pitched one and the landmark spire added. The church received the first organ donation in Corstorphine when Andrew Carnegie paid the full cost of a new water-driven organ in 1902. A house built in Ladywell Avenue by the first minister, Dr George Burns, was purchased from him by the church in 1859 to serve as the manse, which it did until 1983 when it passed back into private ownership. The garden wall of the Corstorphine Parish Church manse (which gave its name to the adjoining road) runs alongside the second telegraph pole on the right. Most of the trees in the picture were cut down in 1923 for road widening, but nonetheless this is still a traffic bottleneck today.

This view of St John's Road, taken closer to Clermiston Road than the previous one, looks eastwards at a time when there was no problem with traffic-flow: here the only vehicle in sight is a one horsepower cart. The Harp Inn occupied the premises on the extreme left, beyond which was Dickson's Coach Hire (later Garage), then the Oak Inn. Amongst the shops in the middle distance were Thomson's the fishmonger, a branch of the Union Bank and Turner's hardware store. The ground on which the Oak Inn (established c.1851) now stands was leased for development by Sir Robert Dick in 1825 to David Cuddie, postmaster. The Harp Inn was built shortly afterwards and bears the date of 1826. The old parish church was formerly dedicated to St John the Baptist and it is this saint who gave his name to St John's Road. It is certain that before John lost his head at King Herod's command and Salome's request, he would never have dreamt that 1,800 years later a wee place called Corstorphine would apply his name to its new main road. Then, to cap that, the Roman Catholic chapel would resurrect his name yet again, for their place of worship in St Ninian's Road.

This group of shops with flats above them on the south side of St John's Road is known as Ormiston Terrace. The terrace was built in 1885 by Charles and Thomas Blaikie, who operated a grocery business, and was named after their mother, Matilda Ormiston. It is not uncommon for an individual terrace or short section of road to have a different name from the more major road of which it forms a part, and several examples exist within the areas covered by this book.

The foot of Clermiston Road, the east side of which was given the name Belgrave Terrace when the tenements were erected in 1903. Braefoot Dairy had several owners over the years of its existence (including Mr Dickson, who ran the garage a few doors along the road) and in this postcard Mr Liddle is the proprietor. Almost a century after this postcard was produced a hairdresser occupies the premises.

A busy scene on Clermiston Road at its junction with Forrester Road (left) and Belgrave Road. Home deliveries were being made by local commercial concerns when the photograph was taken, and a variety of early forms of transport can be seen. Clermiston Road follows the line of an ancient thoroughfare up and over Corstorphine Hill.

G. G. W. – C.

The Victorian mansion of Clerwood House was built *c*.1860 with wonderful views to the south and west. It was home to the Tod family, owners of a flour-milling business prior to the Second World War. The Tods were extremely interested in the social and spiritual welfare of the local community, and Mr T. W. Tod helped finance St Anne's Church in 1903. After the First World War his eldest daughter, Miss Margaret (Peggy) Tod was involved not only in founding but also funding the Corstorphine Village Institute. Its hall was erected in 1920, close to where the Centurion Inn is now located at the top of Featherhall Avenue, and she equipped it with billiard tables and other facilities. It soon became a very popular venue used by diverse groups including ex-servicemen, Boy Scouts and the Women's Institute. Clerwood House was later converted to a children's home and is presently occupied by the General Teaching Council for Scotland. In 1924 Margaret gained first class honours in medicine at Edinburgh University and won the Ettles Scholarship, the first woman ever to do so. A faithful servant to Corstorphine throughout her life, she died on 26 July 1953.

St Ninian's Road, Corstorphine

239/17.

Developed by 1903, St Ninian's Road took its name from the altar of St Ninian in the old parish church. This in turn was named after the early Christian missionary from Whithorn, who was later canonised. In 1929 the nearby United Free Church obtained its new appellation from this road, an appropriate choice given the religious relevance of the saint's name to the area. The young lady who sent this card in 1915 mentions that she has had 'a touch of toothache but I have got them drawn so they will trouble me no more'. Dentists did not waste time with fillings in those days!

Victor Park Terrace was developed during the very last years of the nineteenth century on the old Ferrygate, which may derive from the Anglo–Saxon *fergen gata*, meaning hill path. Closed sometime between 1746 and 1752, this road once led to Clermiston Hill and Cramond Muir (Drumbrae) and on to South Queensferry. It was believed to be part of a route used by pilgrims who wished to call at the parish church and Our Lady's Well on their pilgrimage from Whithorn (home of St Ninian) to Tain. Charles Victor Parker, who later owned the land, gave his name to the new terrace, whilst the houses on the right were called Maybank Villas. At the foot of this view of Victor Park Terrace, green fields stretch all the way to the Pentlands, making quite a contrast with the same scene today.

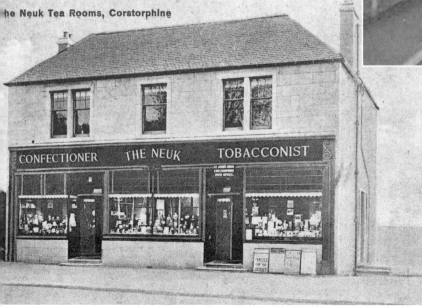

he Neuk Tea Rooms, Corstorphine

In the years after the First World War a single-storey building housed The Neuk tearooms. This was located on the western edge of the village and provided refreshments for hikers and cyclists journeying into the surrounding countryside. The original building was subsequently replaced by the present two-storey structure, which provided room for Corstorphine post office, situated in the right-hand half of the building. Outside, the *Daily Sketch* poster advertises 'Funeral Pictures' whilst another board reads 'Fancies for the Derby'. This postcard, sent in November 1942, was published by E. C. Frier, Neuk Tea Rooms. McColl's shop currently occupies the entire ground floor of the building, although the post office is still contained within it, at the rear of the premises.

This photograph of Corstorphine Rangers football team, taken during the 1910–11 season, includes quite a few well-known Corstorphine family names. Many of the players earned their livings as local tradesmen. At the beginning of the twentieth century there were few proper grounds for amateur teams, and instead football was played wherever there was a suitable open area. The construction of St Anne's Church in 1903 removed one popular venue from the list of playing fields.

Back row: A. Robertson, W. Steedman, R. Glendinning, A. Arthur, P. Burnet, A. Bowick, A. Kilgour (Committee)

Middle row: D. B. Campbell (President), A. Steedman, L. Riddle, G. Paterson, G. Rae, J. Forrest, M. Calder, G. Gilroy, M. McLeish, G. Donaldson (Secretary)

Front row: J. Wallace (Vice-President), A. Hossack, A. McIntosh, J. Wight (Captain), W. Scobbie, W. Kidd, A. Dickson (President Scottish Junior Football Association).